W9-CLN-070

NEW MEXICO

BY ALICIA Z. KLEPEIS

BELLWETHER MEDIA • MINNEAPOLIS, MN

Blastoff! Discovery launches a new mission: reading to learn. Filled with facts and features, each book offers you an exciting new world to explore!

BLASTOFF! UNIVERSE

BLASTOFF! Beginners — GRADE K

BLASTOFF! READERS — GRADES 1-3

BLASTOFF! DISCOVERY — GRADE 4

This edition first published in 2022 by Bellwether Media, Inc.

No part of this publication may be reproduced in whole or in part without written permission of the publisher.
For information regarding permission, write to Bellwether Media, Inc., Attention: Permissions Department,
6012 Blue Circle Drive, Minnetonka, MN 55343.

Library of Congress Cataloging-in-Publication Data

Names: Klepeis, Alicia, 1971- author.
Title: New Mexico / by Alicia Z. Klepeis.
Other titles: Blastoff! discovery. State profiles.
Description: Minneapolis, MN : Bellwether Media, Inc., 2022. | Series: Blastoff! discovery : state profiles | Includes bibliographical references and index. | Audience: Ages 7-13 | Audience: Grades 4-6 | Summary: "Engaging images accompany information about New Mexico. The combination of high-interest subject matter and narrative text is intended for students in grades 3 through 8"–Provided by publisher.
Identifiers: LCCN 2021019651 (print) | LCCN 2021019652 (ebook) | ISBN 9781644873366 (library binding) | ISBN 9781648341793 (ebook)
Subjects: LCSH: New Mexico–Juvenile literature. | CYAC: New Mexico. | LCGFT: Instructional and educational works.
Classification: LCC F796.3 .K55 2022 (print) | LCC F796.3 (ebook) | DDC 978.9–dc23
LC record available at https://lccn.loc.gov/2021019651
LC ebook record available at https://lccn.loc.gov/2021019652

Editor: Betsy Rathburn   Designer: Andrea Schneider

Printed in the United States of America, North Mankato, MN.

TABLE OF CONTENTS

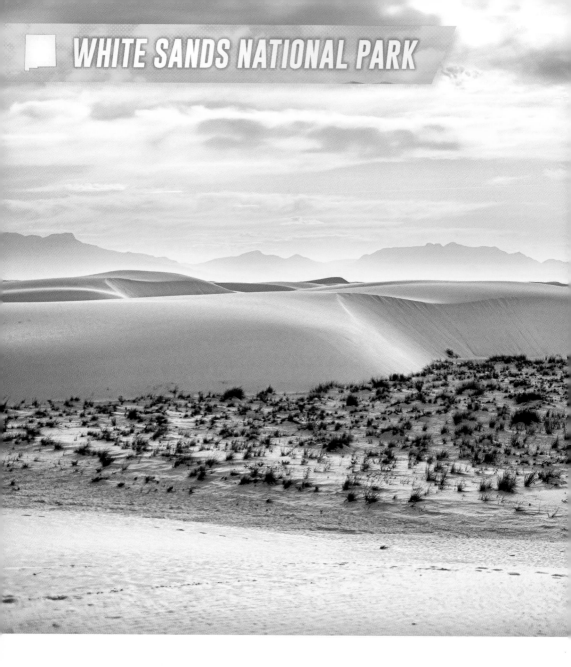

A family drives into White Sands National Park on a warm fall morning. They stop at the visitor center and watch a film about the park's landscape. On a walking tour, the family explores the plants of the Chihuahuan Desert. Yucca trees and skunkbush sumac thrive under the hot sun.

BANDELIER NATIONAL MONUMENT

KASHA-KATUWE TENT ROCKS NATIONAL MONUMENT

SHIPROCK PEAK

TAOS PUEBLO

WHITE SANDS NATIONAL PARK
TULAROSA BASIN

After a short drive past fields of rolling **gypsum** hills, the family parks at a trailhead. With sleds in hand, they hike up a steep **dune**. Then they slide down it. They spend the afternoon climbing up and sledding down. An orange sunset lights the park as they leave. Welcome to New Mexico!

UTAH

New Mexico is in the southwestern United States. Its land stretches over 121,590 square miles (314,917 square kilometers). The Sangre de Cristo Mountains stand in north-central New Mexico over Santa Fe, the state capital. West of Santa Fe, the Rio Grande flows southward through the middle of the state. Its waters pass through Albuquerque, New Mexico's biggest city.

Arizona lies to the west of New Mexico. New Mexico's northern neighbor is Colorado. Oklahoma shares a small border with New Mexico in the northeast. Texas borders New Mexico both to the east and the southeast. New Mexico's southwestern neighbor is Mexico.

ARIZONA

MEXICO

COLORADO

OKLAHOMA —

★

SANTA FE

RIO RANCHO ●
● ALBUQUERQUE

NEW MEXICO

ROSWELL
●

RIO GRANDE

● LAS CRUCES

TEXAS

FOUR CORNERS

Four Corners Monument is shared
between New Mexico, Colorado,
Utah, and Arizona. It is the only place
in the U.S. where four states meet!

LAGUNA *PUEBLO*

People first came to New Mexico more than 10,000 years ago. In time, Native American tribes formed. They included the Pueblo, Navajo, and Apache. Spanish explorers arrived in New Mexico in 1540. The area became a Spanish **colony** in 1595. In 1821, it became part of Mexico.

New Mexico became a U.S. **territory** in the mid-19th century. It became the 47th state in 1912. Today, most Native Americans in New Mexico live on one of the state's **reservations**. Some live in one of the state's 19 *pueblos*. These **traditional** villages of the Pueblo people are many centuries old.

NATIVE PEOPLES OF NEW MEXICO

NAVAJO

- Original lands in northwestern New Mexico
- About 106,800 members in New Mexico today

PUEBLO

- Original lands in northwestern and north-central New Mexico
- 19 Pueblo tribes
- More than 50,000 live in New Mexico's pueblo villages, with others living throughout New Mexico

APACHE

- Three Apache tribes in New Mexico: Fort Sill, Jicarilla, and Mescalero
- Original lands in southwestern New Mexico (Fort Sill), northern New Mexico (Jicarilla), and south-central New Mexico (Mescalero)

Northwestern New Mexico is home to the Colorado **Plateau**. This area is full of cliffs, **mesas**, and deep **canyons**. The Rocky Mountains run through north-central New Mexico. The Basin and Range region covers central and southwestern New Mexico. The Rio Grande flows through this area. The Great Plains sweep across eastern New Mexico. The Chihuahuan Desert covers much of the south.

— RIO GRANDE

N
W E
S

COLORADO PLATEAU
CHIHUAHUAN DESERT

RIO GRANDE

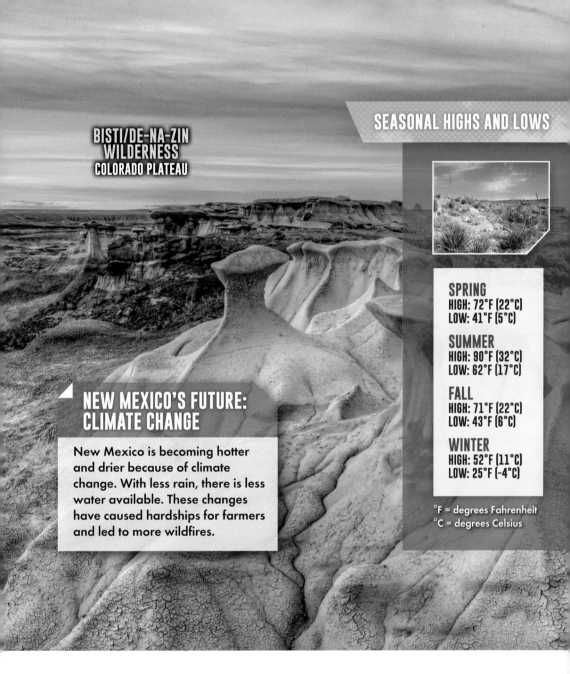

BISTI/DE-NA-ZIN
WILDERNESS
COLORADO PLATEAU

SPRING
HIGH: 72°F (22°C)
LOW: 41°F (5°C)

SUMMER
HIGH: 90°F (32°C)
LOW: 62°F (17°C)

FALL
HIGH: 71°F (22°C)
LOW: 43°F (6°C)

WINTER
HIGH: 52°F (11°C)
LOW: 25°F (-4°C)

°F = degrees Fahrenheit
°C = degrees Celsius

NEW MEXICO'S FUTURE: CLIMATE CHANGE

New Mexico is becoming hotter and drier because of climate change. With less rain, there is less water available. These changes have caused hardships for farmers and led to more wildfires.

New Mexico has a warm, dry climate. Mountainous areas get more rain. Temperatures are cooler in the mountains, too. Wildfires sometimes burn forests throughout New Mexico.

11

MOUNTAIN LION

New Mexico has a rich variety of wildlife. Mountain lions stalk bighorn sheep and mule deer in the mountains and forests. Coyotes live across the state. They feed on anything from fruit and seeds to rabbits and mice. Greater roadrunners chase down rattlesnakes in the Chihuahuan Desert. Whiptail lizards scurry about in search of termites and other insects on the desert floor.

GREATER ROADRUNNER

New Mexico has hundreds of bird species. Turkey vultures soar through the desert skies. Burrowing owls dig underground homes throughout the state. Colorful western tanagers fly through wooded areas.

WESTERN WHIPTAIL LIZARD

BURROWING OWL

TURKEY VULTURE

WESTERN TANAGER

Life Span: up to 15 years
Status: least concern

western tanager range =

LEAST CONCERN	NEAR THREATENED	VULNERABLE	ENDANGERED	CRITICALLY ENDANGERED	EXTINCT IN THE WILD	EXTINCT

More than 2 million people live in New Mexico. Around 3 out of 4 New Mexicans live in **urban** areas. The largest cities are Albuquerque, Las Cruces, Rio Rancho, and Santa Fe.

LAS CRUCES

SANTA FE

SUSANA MARTINEZ

On January 1, 2011, Susana Martinez was sworn into office as the first female governor of New Mexico. She served for two terms.

FAMOUS NEW MEXICAN

Name: Neil Patrick Harris
Born: June 15, 1973
Hometown: Albuquerque, New Mexico
Famous For: Award-winning actor known for TV shows including *A Series of Unfortunate Events* and movies such as *The Smurfs* and *Cloudy With a Chance of Meatballs*

Almost half of New Mexicans are Hispanic. People with European **ancestors** make up the second-largest group. About 1 out of 10 New Mexicans has Native American **heritage**. Smaller groups of New Mexicans are Asian American or Black or African American. Many **immigrants** live in New Mexico. Most come from Mexico. Others are from the Philippines, India, Germany, and Cuba.

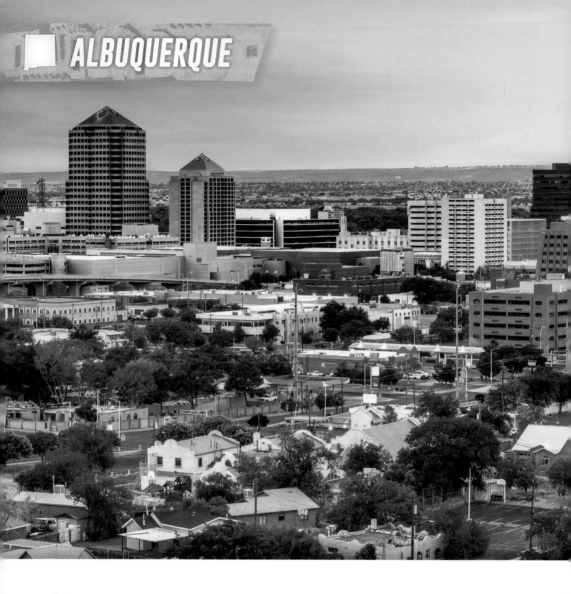

Native Americans lived in New Mexico's Rio Grande Valley for thousands of years. They built homes, grew crops, and created art. In 1706, European settlers founded a city in the area. They named it Albuquerque. Albuquerque became an important city for trade. It is still a business and transportation **hub** today.

Albuquerque is also a **cultural** center. Visitors to the Albuquerque Museum take in performances and explore paintings and sculptures. The ABQ BioPark draws visitors with its zoo, garden, and aquarium. The Indian Pueblo Cultural Center includes art and history displays to teach about the Pueblo people.

ZUNI PUEBLO DANCERS
INDIAN PUEBLO CULTURAL CENTER

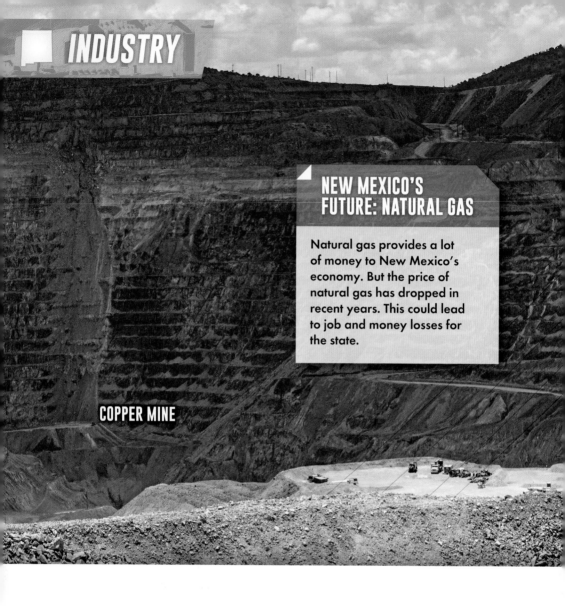

NEW MEXICO'S FUTURE: NATURAL GAS

Natural gas provides a lot of money to New Mexico's economy. But the price of natural gas has dropped in recent years. This could lead to job and money losses for the state.

COPPER MINE

In its early days, New Mexico's economy was based on **agriculture**. Cattle and dairy are still important today. Mining also brings in a lot of money. Companies mine for copper, gold, and silver. Other **natural resources**, such as oil and gas, are also found in New Mexico.

Tourism is New Mexico's largest industry. People working in tourism may hold **service jobs** at national parks or hotels. Other New Mexicans have jobs in the government or the military. Factories also employ many people. They often make electronic equipment and computer parts.

INVENTED IN NEW MEXICO

ALTAIR 8800 MICROCOMPUTER KIT

Date Invented: 1974

Inventor: Henry Edward Roberts

ATOMIC BOMB

Date Invented: early 1940s

Inventor: J. Robert Oppenheimer

BREAKFAST BURRITO

Date Invented: 1970s

Inventor: Tia Sophia's restaurant

FRITO PIE

Date Invented: 1960s

Inventor: Teresa Hernandez

CHILES RELLENOS

New Mexican foods often have Mexican origins. Tacos and guacamole are common favorites. Green chile peppers are used in many dishes, such as *chiles rellenos*. This tasty dish is made of chiles stuffed with cheese or meat, then breaded and fried. Green chile stew features spicy chiles and pork or beef.

RED OR GREEN?

Food in New Mexican restaurants is often served with red or green chile sauce. People who want both sauces ask for "Christmas"!

20

Blue corn is a traditional Native American food. Sweeter than yellow corn, it is used in pancakes and a hot drink called *atole*. Piñon nuts grow on New Mexico's state tree, the piñon. People use them in candies and cakes. They are even used to flavor coffee!

GREEN CHILE STEW

ATOLE

GUACAMOLE

Guacamole is a common side to many favorite dishes in New Mexico. Have an adult help you make this recipe.

INGREDIENTS

3 avocados with peels and pits removed

1 lime, juiced

1 teaspoon salt

1/2 cup diced onion

3 tablespoons chopped fresh cilantro

2 Roma tomatoes, diced

1 teaspoon minced garlic

DIRECTIONS

1. In a medium bowl, mash together the avocados, lime juice, and salt.

2. Mix in the onion, cilantro, tomatoes, and garlic.

3. Refrigerate for 1 hour, or serve immediately with tortilla chips.

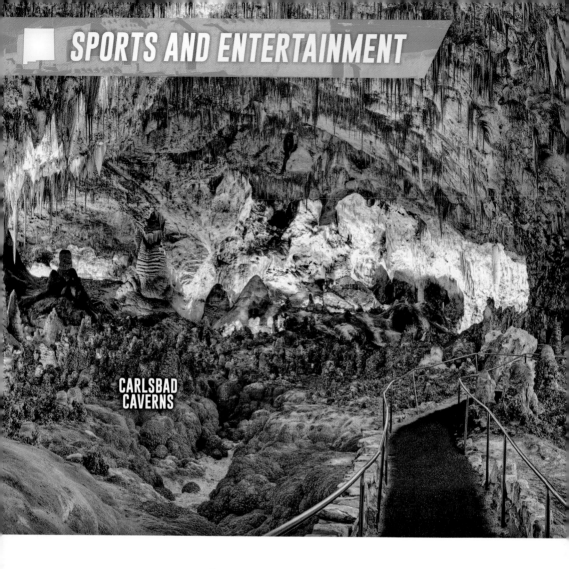

CARLSBAD
CAVERNS

Many New Mexicans love sports. Baseball fans cheer for the Albuquerque Isotopes. College football fans often root for the New Mexico Lobos. Outdoor activities are also popular in New Mexico. The Carlsbad Caverns draw cave explorers. People boat and fish at Elephant Butte Lake State Park. In the winter, skiing and snowboarding are common in the mountains.

Art is also popular in New Mexico. Colorful sculptures make the Meow Wolf Art Complex a fun place to visit. The Museum of Indian Arts and Culture shows off past and present Native American art. Concerts and theater performances draw many visitors to New Mexico's cities.

MEOW WOLF ART COMPLEX

NOTABLE SPORTS TEAM

Albuquerque Isotopes
Sport: Minor League Baseball
Started: 2003
Place of Play: Rio Grande Credit Union Field at Isotopes Park

New Mexico is a land of celebrations. Every April, the Gathering of Nations is held in Albuquerque. Thousands gather to enjoy a traditional Native American **powwow**. It is the largest powwow in the world! In July, the city of Roswell holds the alien-themed UFO Festival. Events include costume contests, a car show, and a parade. The Fiesta de Santa Fe has taken place since 1712. Live music and arts and crafts are part of this September event.

Every October, hundreds of hot-air balloons fill the sky during the International Balloon Fiesta in Albuquerque. People come from around the world to take in the colorful event. New Mexicans celebrate their traditions all year long!

GATHERING OF NATIONS POWWOW

INTERNATIONAL
BALLOON FIESTA
ALBUQUERQUE

AROUND 700

The first Pueblo villages are built in New Mexico

BETWEEN 1607 AND 1610

Santa Fe is founded

1821

The region of New Mexico becomes part of Mexico

1540

Francisco Vásquez de Coronado explores New Mexico

1706

Albuquerque is founded

1912

New Mexico becomes
the 47th state

2011

Susana Martinez begins
serving as New Mexico's
first female governor

1945

The world's first
atomic bomb is
tested in Los Alamos

2019

White Sands becomes
a national park

1848

The Treaty of Guadalupe Hidalgo ends the
Mexican-American War, giving the U.S.
control of much of present-day New Mexico

Population

2,117,522
(2020)

Nicknames: Land of Enchantment

Motto: *Crescit Enudo* (It Grows As It Goes)

Date of Statehood: January 6, 1912
(the 47th state)

Capital City: Santa Fe ⭐

Other Major Cities: Albuquerque, Las Cruces, Rio Rancho

Area: 121,590 square miles (314,917 square kilometers);
New Mexico is the 5th largest state.

STATE FLAG

The background of New Mexico's flag is yellow. In the center of the flag is a red design. It is a symbol for the sun used by the Zia Pueblo people. The red and yellow colors are based on an old design of Spain's flag.

INDUSTRY

Main Exports

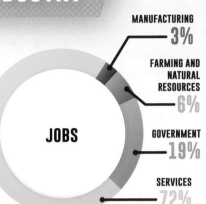

JOBS

- MANUFACTURING **3%**
- FARMING AND NATURAL RESOURCES **6%**
- GOVERNMENT **19%**
- SERVICES **72%**

computer parts | **electronic equipment** | **tree nuts**

dairy products | **beef**

Natural Resources
oil, coal, natural gas, copper, potash

GOVERNMENT

Federal Government
3 REPRESENTATIVES | **2** SENATORS

NM

5 ELECTORAL VOTES

USA

State Government
70 REPRESENTATIVES | **42** SENATORS

STATE SYMBOLS

STATE BIRD
GREATER ROADRUNNER

STATE ANIMAL
BLACK BEAR

STATE FLOWER
YUCCA FLOWER

STATE TREE
PIÑON

agriculture—the practice of raising crops and animals

ancestors—relatives who lived long ago

canyons—narrow, deep valleys that have steep sides

colony—a distant territory which is under the control of another nation

cultural—relating to the beliefs, arts, and ways of life in a place or society

dune—a hill made of sand or other fine, loose material

gypsum—a colorless mineral often used to improve soil

heritage—the traditions, achievements, and beliefs that are part of the history of a group of people

hub—a center of activity

immigrants—people who move to a new country

mesas—flat-topped hills

natural resources—materials in the earth that are taken out and used to make products or fuel

plateau—an area of flat, raised land

powwow—a Native American gathering that usually includes dancing

reservations—areas of land that are controlled by Native American tribes

service jobs—jobs that perform tasks for people or businesses

territory—an area of land under the control of a government; territories in the United States are considered part of the country but do not have power in the government.

tourism—the business of people traveling to visit other places

traditional—related to customs, ideas, or beliefs handed down from one generation to the next

urban—related to cities and city life

AT THE LIBRARY

Bodden, Valerie. *Apache*. Mankato, Minn.: Creative Education, 2018.

Burgan, Michael. *New Mexico*. New York, N.Y.: Children's Press, 2019.

Murray, Julie. *New Mexico*. Minneapolis, Minn.: Big Buddy Books, 2020.

ON THE WEB

Factsurfer.com gives you a safe, fun way to find more information.

1. Go to www.factsurfer.com.

2. Enter "New Mexico" into the search box and click 🔍.

3. Select your book cover to see a list of related content.

INDEX

The images in this book are reproduced through the courtesy of: Nick Fox, front cover, pp. 2–3; etorres, p. 3 (tacos); Andriy Blokhin, pp. 4–5 (White Sands National Park); Traveller70, p. 5 (Bandelier National Monument, Kasha-Katuwe Tent Rocks National Monument); Sean Pavone, pp. 5 (Shiprock Peak), 14 (Santa Fe), 16, 19 (background); Gimas, pp. 5 (Taos Pueblo), 9; Natalia Bratslavsky, p. 8 (Laguna Pueblo); Hank Shiffman, p. 10 (Rio Grande); Colin D. Young, p. 11 (Bisti/De-Na-Zin Wilderness); Martina Roth, p. 11 (inset); FotoRequest, p. 12 (turkey vulture); Warren Metcalf, p. 12 (mountain lion); Dennis W Donohue, p. 12 (greater roadrunner); reptiles4all, p. 12 (western whiptail lizard); Albert Beukhof, p. 12 (burrowing owl); Eivor Kuchta, p. 12 (western tanager); Eric James/ Alamy, p. 14 (Las Cruces); Wikipedia, pp. 14 (Susana Martinez), 19 (ALTAIR 8800); Album/ Alamy, p. 15 (background); Kathy Hutchins, p. 15 (Neil Patrick Harris); Kit Leong, p. 17; Underawesternsky, p. 18; Francesco Milanese, p. 19 (atomic bomb); ImagePixel, p. 19 (breakfast burrito); Brent Hofacker, p. 19 (Frito pie); lunamarina, p. 20 (chiles rellenos); pixshots, p. 20 (chile sauce); Solaria/ Alamy, p. 20 (green chile sauce); Lemonpink Images, p. 20 (atole); alisafarov, p. 20 (guacamole background); vitals, p. 20 (guacamole); Doug Meek, p. 20 (Carlsbad Caverns); David L. Moore - US SW/ Alamy, p. 23 (Meow Wolf Art Complex); Cal Sport Media/ Alamy, p. 23 (Albuquerque Isotopes); Maks Narodenko, p. 23 (baseball); ZUMA Press Inc/ Alamy, pp. 24 (Gathering of Nations), 27 (2011); Steve Bower, pp. 24–25 (International Balloon Fiesta); Dean Fikar, pp. 26–27, 28–29, 30–31, 32; Janice and Nolan Braud/ Alamy, p. 26 (1706); Lefteris Papaulakis, p. 27 (1912); Richard A McMillin, p. 27 (2019); Nicku, p. 28 (flag); Dennis W Donohue, p. 29 (greater roadrunner); BGSmith, p. 29 (black bear); sumikophoto, p. 29 (yucca flower); Sabrina Imperi, p. 29 (piñon); Mircea Costina, p. 31 (hot-air balloon).